Clifton Park - Halfmoon Pul

W9-BCN-831

WINTER OLYMPIC SPORTS

PARALYMPIC SPORTS EVENTS

by Robin Johnson

Words that are defined in the glossary are in **bold** type the first time they appear in the text.

A table of abbreviations used for the names of countries appears on page 32.

Crabtree editor: Adrianna Morganelli
Proofreader: Crystal Sikkens
Editorial director: Kathy Middleton
Production coordinator and
   prepress technician: Katherine Berti
Developed for Crabtree Publishing Company by
RJF Publishing LLC (www.RJFpublishing.com)
Editor: Jacqueline Laks Gorman
Designer: Tammy West, Westgraphix LLC
Photo Researcher: Edward A. Thomas
Indexer: Nila Glikin

Photo Credits:
Associated Press: Wide World Photos: p. 8
Gigi Arcaini/epa/Corbis: p. 28
Getty Images: p. 2, 4, 7, 12, 13, 14, 18, 19, 22,
   24, 26; AFP: p. 6, 15, 16, 23; Bongarts:
   front cover, p. 20, 25
Tony Gentile/Reuters/Landov: p. 10, 11

Cover: Liudmila Vauchok of Belarus in cross-country
skiing competition at the 2006 Winter Paralympic Games.

CONTENTS

Library and Archives Canada Cataloguing in Publication

Johnson, Robin (Robin R.)
   Paralympic sports events / Robin Johnson.

(Winter Olympic sports)   2252
Includes index.
ISBN 978-0-7787-4025-4 (bound).--ISBN 978-0-7787-4044-5 (pbk.)

   1. Paralympics--Juvenile literature. 2. Sports for people with
disabilities--Juvenile literature. 3. Winter Olympics--Juvenile
literature. I. Title. II. Series: Winter Olympic sports

GV722.5.P37J64 2009   j796.04'56   C2009-903222-8

Library of Congress Cataloging-in-Publication Data

Johnson, Robin (Robin R.)
   Paralympic sports events / Robin Johnson.
      p. cm. -- (Winter Olympic sports)
   Includes index.

   ISBN 978-0-7787-4044-5 (pbk. : alk. paper)
-- ISBN 978-0-7787-4025-4 (reinforced library binding : alk. paper)
   1. Paralympics. 2. Athletes with disabilities. I. Title.

   GV183.5.J65 2010
   796.04'56--dc22

                              2009021497

Crabtree Publishing Company
www.crabtreebooks.com   1-800-387-7650

Published in Canada	**Published in the United States**	**Published in the United Kingdom**	**Published in Australia**
Crabtree Publishing	Crabtree Publishing	Crabtree Publishing	Crabtree Publishing
616 Welland Ave.	PMB16A	White Cross Mills	386 Mt. Alexander Rd.
St. Catharines, ON	350 Fifth Ave., Suite 3308	High Town, Lancaster	Ascot Vale (Melbourne)
L2M 5V6	New York, NY 10118	LA1 4XS	VIC 3032

THE PARALYMPIC GAMES

The Paralympic Games are a series of sporting events in which highly skilled athletes with physical disabilities compete against other athletes with similar disabilities. The motto for the Games is "Spirit in Motion."

Michael Milton (AUS) skis to a gold medal in the super-G at the 2002 Paralympic Winter Games.

WHAT'S IN A NAME?

The name *Paralympics* is a combination of the words *para*—which means "alongside"—and *Olympics*. The event got its name because the Paralympic Games have always been held in the same year as the Olympic Games.

DID YOU KNOW?

The Paralympics have not always been held in the same city as the Olympic Games. The first Paralympic Winter Games to be held in the same city as the Winter Olympics were the 1992 Games, in Albertville, France.

LET THE GAMES BEGIN!

The 2010 Paralympic Winter Games will be held in and around Vancouver, Canada, in March 2010, about two weeks after the Olympic Winter Games have ended.

SOMETHING SPECIAL

The Paralympics should not be confused with Special Olympic World Games, an international sporting competition for people with intellectual disabilities.

SUPER STATS

About 250 athletes competed in the first Paralympic Winter Games. In 2010, about 600 athletes are expected to compete.

Russia won the most medals of any nation at the 2006 Winter Paralympics, with a total of 33. Russia also won the most gold medals—13.

OLYMPICS FACT FILE

- In 1948, a doctor named Sir Ludwig Guttman began using sports to help **rehabilitate** injured World War II veterans at England's Stoke Mandeville Hospital. He organized a sporting competition—which was held on the opening day of the 1948 Summer Olympics—for his patients.

- In 1952, athletes from the Netherlands joined the sporting event, and it became the first international competition of its kind.

- In 1960, the first Olympic-type competition for athletes with disabilities was held in Rome, Italy. The event was called the Stoke Mandeville Games. The name was later changed to the Paralympic Summer Games.

- In 1976, the first Paralympic Winter Games took place in the city of Örnsköldsvik, Sweden.

- The Paralympics have always followed the Olympic schedule, now alternating between Summer and Winter Games every two years. Since 1988, Paralympic events have also been contested at the same venues as Olympic events.

Muffy Davis (USA), competing on a sit-ski, in action at the 2002 Games.

ALPINE SKIING EVENTS

Competitors in **alpine** events ski down steep, snowy mountains at high speeds. Racers compete in men's or women's events in one of three classes—standing, sitting, and **visually impaired**.

WHISTLE WHILE YOU SKI

At the 2010 Paralympic Winter Games, alpine skiing events—downhill, slalom, giant slalom, super-G, and super combined—will take place in Whistler, British Columbia. All events will run on the same courses used in the 2010 Olympic women's skiing competitions.

GEAR UP!

Alpine racers use long, narrow skis and carry thin, lightweight poles for balance and power. The poles used for downhill and super-G are curved, so that they fit around the body. In contrast, the poles used for slalom and giant slalom are straight. Standing alpine competitors may use the same equipment as able-bodied skiers, or they may ski with **prostheses** and stabilizers. Sitting skiers compete on sit-skis. They—as well as some standing skiers—may also use outriggers. Visually impaired competitors use standard ski equipment but race near able-bodied guides.

TECHNICALLY SPEEDING

There are two types of alpine events—speed and technical. Speed events challenge racers to maintain control while skiing quickly down steep mountain courses. Technical events require skiers to complete difficult maneuvers at high speeds. Alpine skiers often compete in both types of events at the Paralympic Games.

THE IPC IN CHARGE

The Paralympic movement is governed by the International Paralympic Committee (IPC), with headquarters in Germany. The IPC organizes both the Summer and Winter Paralympic Games, as well as running World Championships and other athletic competitions.

LEARN THE LINGO

Guide—a **sighted** skier who uses voice commands or radios to direct a visually impaired racer through the skiing course

Outrigger—a pole with a short ski blade on the end that helps a skier balance

Sit-ski—a specially made chair with seat belts and straps on a single ski; also called a mono-ski

Stabilizer—a crutch with a small ski on the end, used instead of a ski pole

DRESS FOR SUCCESS

Alpine skiers wear lightweight, body-hugging ski suits, protective helmets and goggles, and hard, supportive boots that attach to skis at the toe and heel. Slalom skiers often wear pads. These help protect them from injury as they ski down the slalom course.

DOWNHILL

The downhill event **debuted** at the 1984 Paralympic Winter Games, and it's been all downhill since then!

Canada's Stacy William Kohut competes in the 1998 men's sitting downhill event.

DOWNHILL 101

Downhill is a speed event. Competitors race against the clock as they ski down a long, steep course with jumps and turns but fewer gates than the other alpine events.

2006 PARALYMPIC CHAMPIONS: MEN: SITTING: KEVIN BRAMBLE (USA)
STANDING: GERD SCHÖNFELDER (GER)   VISUALLY IMPAIRED: GERD GRADWOHL (GER)

Jacob Rife (USA) skis to a bronze medal in the men's 2002 standing downhill.

RACE BASICS

Each competitor makes a single run down the course — the longest of all the alpine events. The racer with the fastest time skis away with the gold medal.

DISQUALIFIED!

Competitors must ski between a series of thin, flexible poles called gates on all alpine courses. A skier who misses a gate is **disqualified** from the race.

NEED FOR SPEED

Downhill races are the fastest alpine events, reaching speeds of more than 62 MPH (100 km/h)!

QUICK SILVERS

At the 2002 Games, Muffy Davis (USA) helped the United States sweep the **podium** in three out of the four women's sitting events. Davis — who has had **paraplegia** since a skiing accident in 1989 — won silver medals in the women's downhill, giant slalom, and super-G events.

DOWN THE BRAMBLE PATH

The gold medal winner in the downhill sitting event at both the 2002 and 2006 Paralympic Games, Kevin Bramble (USA), was a serious snowboarder until he had an accident that left him paralyzed. He taught himself to mono-ski and was soon winning medals. He also designs, builds, and sells mono-skis.

OH MY GERD!

Gerd Schönfelder (GER) has won more medals in alpine events than any other Paralympian, with an incredible 17 medals to his credit! The legendary skier — who competed in the Games from 1992 through 2006 — has earned 12 gold medals in alpine races, including a **sweep** of the men's standing events in 2002.

BURNING UP THE COURSE

Hans Burn (SUI) was burning up the slopes in the men's alpine standing events from 1988 to 2002. He won a total of 14 medals in downhill, slalom, giant slalom, and super-G, including six golds.

2006 PARALYMPIC CHAMPIONS: WOMEN: SITTING: LAURIE STEPHENS (USA) STANDING: SOLENE JAMBAQUE (FRA) VISUALLY IMPAIRED: PASCALE CASANOVA (FRA)

7

SLALOM

France's Nicolas Berejny (left), accompanied by his guide, skis to victory in the men's visually impaired slalom race in 2006.

Paralympic slalom racers have been zigzagging down mountainsides since the first Winter Games in 1976.

2006 PARALYMPIC CHAMPIONS: MEN: SITTING: MARTIN BRAXENTHALER (GER)
STANDING: ROBERT MEUSBURGER (AUT)   VISUALLY IMPAIRED: NICOLAS BEREJNY (FRA)

SLALOM 101

Slalom is a technical event that requires skiers to make quick, precise turns as they navigate their way through a series of gates. With the shortest course and the most gates, slalom has the fastest, sharpest turns of any alpine event.

RACE BASICS

In slalom events, skiers compete in two races held on the same day. Each race takes place on a different course. The fastest combined time wins the gold medal.

WHAT'S IN A NAME?

The word *slalom* means to ski around obstacles on a zigzag course. It comes from the Norwegian words for "sloping path."

HALL OF FAMER

At the first two Paralympic Winter Games, Germany's Annemie Schneider won every women's alpine event in her standing class. She went on to compete in four more Games and capture three more medals. In 2006, Schneider — an **amputee** — became the first female winter-sport champion to be inducted into the Paralympic Hall of Fame.

THE WONDER FROM DOWN UNDER

When Michael Milton (AUS) won the slalom event in 1992, he became the first Australian to win a gold medal in the Paralympic — or Olympic — Winter Games. Milton, a left-leg amputee, competed in five Paralympics and won a total of 11 medals in alpine standing races, including a sweep of his division at the 2002 Games.

DID YOU KNOW?

Allison Jones (USA), the winner of the gold medal in the women's standing slalom in 2006, juggled two sports while also completing her college degree in engineering. She won a silver medal in cycling at the 2008 Paralympic Summer Games.

FIRST MEDAL WINNERS

When the slalom was first held at the 1976 Paralympic Winter Games, nine skiers raced to victory in the different classes. The men's winners were Franz Meister (AUT), Eugen Diethelm (SUI), Heinz Moser (SUI), John Gow (CAN), and Felix Gisler (SUI). The women's winners were Annemie Schneider (FRG), Irene Moillen (SUI), Eva Lemezova (CZE), and Petra Merkott (FRG).

VICTORY FOR VICTOR

Stephani Victor (USA), who won the women's sitting slalom at the 2006 Games, was named *Ski Racing Magazine's* Disabled Athlete of the Year in 2007. She was a film student and actress in 1995, when an out-of-control car hit her, leading to a double amputation of her legs. She worked hard at rehabilitation and took skiing lessons, which led her to the podium.

2006 PARALYMPIC CHAMPIONS: WOMEN: SITTING: STEPHANI VICTOR (USA)
STANDING: ALLISON JONES (USA)   VISUALLY IMPAIRED: PASCALE CASANOVA (FRA)

9

GIANT SLALOM

Giant slalom is one of the original events of the Paralympic Winter Games. It debuted in 1976 and has met with giant success.

Sandy Dukat (USA) in action during the women's giant slalom at the 2006 Paralympic Winter Games.

GIANT SLALOM 101

Giant slalom is a technical race. It is similar to the slalom event but has a longer course and fewer, wider turns.

RACE BASICS

In giant slalom, skiers compete in two races held on the same day. Each race takes place on a different course. Race times are combined to give the competitors their total scores.

2006 PARALYMPIC CHAMPIONS: MEN: STANDING: GERD SCHÖNFELDER (GER) SITTING: MARTIN BRAXENTHALER (GER) VISUALLY IMPAIRED: NICOLAS BEREJNY (FRA)

CLASS ACTS

Competitors in giant slalom—and all other Paralympic ski event—are grouped according to their disabilities. In alpine events, there are three classes for sitting athletes, seven classes for standing athletes, and three classes for visually impaired athletes. Judges use both the times and class rankings of competitors to determine the overall standings in ski events.

GOLDEN GIRL

Lauren Woolstencroft (CAN) earned the nickname "golden girl" for winning a trio of gold medals in Paralympic alpine events. Woolstencroft—who was born missing her left arm below the elbow and both legs below the knees—won the standing slalom and super-G events in 2002 and the giant slalom event in 2006.

V.I.P.

Eric Villalon (ESP) began his Paralympic career in 1998, capturing gold in the men's visually impaired giant slalom, slalom, and super-G events. He went on to complete his medal collection with another six prizes—two gold, three silver, and a bronze—at the 2002 and 2006 Games.

FAST LEARNER

Just three years after he took his first mono-ski lesson, Martin Braxenthaler (GER) joined the German national Paralympic ski team. He also went to the 1998 Paralympic Games, where he won a bronze medal in the super-G. He continued his winning ways in 2002, with gold medals in four races—the giant slalom, slalom, downhill, and super-G. He wasn't done yet. In 2006, he captured gold in the giant slalom, slalom, and super-G.

FIRST MEDAL WINNERS

When the giant slalom was first held at the 1976 Paralympic Winter Games, ten skiers raced to victory in the different classes. The women's winners were Annemie Schneider (FRG), Irene Moillen (SUI), Eva Lemezova (CZE), Elisabeth Osterwalder (SUI), and Petra Merkott (FRG). The men's winners were Ulli Helmbold (FRG), Eugen Diethelm (SUI), Heinz Moser (SUI), Bernard Baudean (FRA), and Adolf Hagn (AUT).

Jan Dostal (CZE) during the men's giant slalom, 2006.

2006 PARALYMPIC CHAMPIONS: WOMEN: SITTING: KUNIKO OBINATA (JPN)
STANDING: LAUREN WOOLSTENCROFT (CAN)   VISUALLY IMPAIRED: SILVIA PARENTE (ITA)

11

SUPER-G

Super-G—which stands for super giant slalom—debuted at the 1994 Paralympic Games.

Reinhild Moeller (GER) competes in the women's standing super-G at the 2006 Games.

SUPER-G 101

Super-G is a speed event that combines the quick turns of giant slalom with the fast pace of downhill. The race is run on a mid-length course—longer than slalom and giant slalom, but shorter than downhill. Men must change direction in the race at least 35 times, while women must change direction at least 30 times.

RACE BASICS

In the super-G event, skiers make single runs down a course. The super skier with the fastest time wins the super-G race.

2006 PARALYMPIC CHAMPIONS: MEN: SITTING: MARTIN BRAXENTHALER (GER)
STANDING: WALTER LACKNER (AUT)   VISUALLY IMPAIRED: GIANMARIA DAL MAISTRO (ITA)

At the 2006 Paralympic Games, 55 competitors entered the men's standing super-G, with 50 advancing to the final round. In contrast, only 19 competitors entered the women's standing super-G event.

SUPER WOMAN

Reinhild Moeller (GER) holds the Paralympic record for the most gold medals in alpine events, winning the top spot on the podium 13 times! She has competed in several Games and captured multiple golds in every standing event since her debut in 1984.

YOUNG GUN

Chris Devlin-Young (USA) is the first athlete to win gold medals in two different classes, having won both standing and sitting events at the Paralympic Games. In 1994, he skied with two outriggers and won the men's standing slalom race. In 2002, he returned to the Paralympics, this time with a mono-ski. Devlin-Young sit-skied his way to victory in the men's super-G event, as well as to silver in the downhill.

Chris Devlin-Young (USA) skis to victory in the men's sitting super-G in 2002.

COMING BACK

In 1993, Sarah Billmeier (USA) suffered a severe injury to the stump of her amputated leg during a super-G race. When she recovered, she had only a couple of weeks to train for the 1994 Paralympics. Still, she won gold in the super-G and downhill and silver in the slalom. She retired from competitive skiing—with a total of 13 Paralympic medals—when she was 25 years old and entered medical school. She became a surgeon.

SUPER COMBINED

The super combined event will be contested for the first time at the 2010 Paralympic Winter Games. The event consists of one downhill race and two slalom races run on shorter courses. The competitors with the fastest overall times in the men's and women's events will ski away with the sport's first Paralympic medals.

2006 PARALYMPIC CHAMPIONS: WOMEN: SITTING: LAURIE STEPHENS (USA)
STANDING: SOLENE JAMBAQUE (FRA) VISUALLY IMPAIRED: SABINE GASTEIGER (AUT)

13

Ragnhild Myklebust (NOR) skis to a gold medal in 2002, in the women's 10km sitting cross-country race.

NORDIC SKIING EVENTS

Competitors in Nordic events ski quickly over snow-covered terrain that is mostly flat.

NORDIC 101

There are two Nordic ski sports at the Paralympic Games — cross-country skiing and biathlon. In cross-country skiing, individuals and teams race through short-distance, middle-distance, or long-distance courses. In biathlon events, competitors ski through a series of short courses, stopping between courses to shoot at targets. Paralympians often compete in both cross country and biathlon.

LET THE GAMES BEGIN!

At the 2010 Winter Games, Nordic skiing events will be held at Whistler Paralympic Park.

RACE BASICS

Men and women compete separately in sitting, standing, and visually impaired events. Races have **interval** starts—which means that a different competitor begins a race every 30 seconds. All events are timed to the tenth of a second, and individual times are adjusted based on the disabilities of the competitors.

GEAR UP!

Standing competitors use the same equipment as able-bodied skiers—two long, narrow skis with curved tips and two strong, lightweight poles. Visually impaired racers also use standard equipment, but they ski with sighted guides. Sitting competitors use sit-skis—chairs attached to a pair of skis. (Alpine sit-skis are single skis only.)

KEEPING BUSY

Mikhail Terentiev (RUS) originally trained to become a ski jumper. He was injured, though, and retired—but then returned to competition in the Paralympic Games, competing in both cross country and biathlon at the Winter Games and in rowing and marathon at the Summer Games. At the 1998 Winter Games, he won two silver medals in cross country, as well as a bronze in biathlon. Four years later, he won a gold and two silvers in cross-country skiing. Then, in 2006, he captured a bronze in biathlon. He also became general secretary of his nation's Paralympic Committee.

Germany's Frank Hoefle on his way to victory in a 2002 cross-country race.

DRESS FOR SUCCESS

Nordic skiers wear stretchy, body-hugging suits and boots that are similar to running shoes. The boots attach to skis at the toes only, allowing the skiers' heels to move freely.

21-MEDAL SALUTE

Knut Lundstrøm (NOR) and Frank Hoefle (GER) share the men's record for the most medals in the Paralympic Winter Games, each with a whopping 21 medals in Nordic skiing and other events! Although Hoefle—who is visually impaired—has one gold medal fewer than Lundstrøm, he also has earned three medals in cycling at the Summer Games!

CROSS-COUNTRY SKIING: INDIVIDUAL

Cross-country racers compete in solo events that test their skiing skills and **endurance.**

Canada's Brian McKeever (left), led by his brother Robin (right), skis his way to a gold medal in 2002.

2006 PARALYMPIC CHAMPIONS: MEN: 5 km SITTING: TARAS KRYJANOVSKI (RUS)
5 km STANDING: STEVEN COOK (USA)   5 km VISUALLY IMPAIRED: BRIAN MCKEEVER (CAN)
10 km SITTING: TARAS KRYJANOVSKI (RUS)   10 km STANDING: STEVEN COOK (USA)
10 km VISUALLY IMPAIRED: BRIAN MCKEEVER (CAN)   15 km SITTING: LURII KOSTIUK (UKR)
20 km STANDING: KIRILL MIKHAYLOV (RUS)   20 km VISUALLY IMPAIRED: OLEH MUNTS (UKR)

SKIING THROUGH THE GAMES

Cross-country skiing debuted at the first Paralympic Winter Games in 1976. That year, men's and women's short-distance individual, middle-distance individual, and **relay** events were held. Cross country has been on the Paralympic program—with different races contested through the years—since then.

RACE BASICS

Individual competitors race against the clock through courses of varying lengths. Men's cross-country events for 2010 are the 1km (0.6 mile) **sprint**, the 10km (6.2 mile) race, the 15km (9.3 mile) race (sitting only), and the 20km (12.4 mile) race (standing and visually impaired only). Women's cross-country events for 2010 are the 1km sprint, the 5km (3.1 mile) race, the 10km race (sitting only), and the 15km race (standing and visually impaired only).

FIRST MEDAL WINNERS

During the 1976 Winter Paralympics, when cross country was first introduced, athletes from the **Scandinavian** countries dominated the competition. Among the men, Finland won 19 of the medals awarded. Swedish women dominated their side, taking 13 medals.

MCKEEVER FEVER

Brian McKeever (CAN)—guided by his older brother (and former Olympian) Robin—has skied his way to seven medals, including four golds, in visually impaired cross-country events. In 2010, he hopes to be the first athlete ever to qualify for both the Paralympic and Olympic Winter Games! (Other athletes with disabilities have competed in the Summer Games.)

DUTCH TREAT

Marjorie van de Bunt (NED), who competes in both cross country and biathlon, won 10 medals at the Winter Paralympics in 1994, 1998, and 2002. She is the only Dutch athlete to win a medal at the Paralympic Winter Games.

CROSS-COUNTRY
SKIING: RELAY

Competitors in action during the sitting portion of the 2006 men's cross-country relay.

In relay events, three-person teams work together to cross the cross-country finish line first.

2006 PARALYMPIC MEDALISTS: MEN: 1 x 3.75km + 2 x 5km RELAY: GOLD: NORWAY   SILVER: RUSSIA   BRONZE: UKRAINE

THREESOME

A cross-country relay race is made up of three legs, or sections. Teammates with different disabilities must ski each leg of the course. Once a skier's entire body has passed the finish line in a leg, the next member of the team can begin to ski his or her leg of the race.

NEAT TECHNIQUES

There are two techniques used in cross-country skiing. In classic technique, competitors keep their skis parallel on a track made by a machine in the snow. In free technique, skiers use the edges of their skis to push themselves forward (like skating). Skiers use different techniques in different cross-country events.

GET A GRIP!

Jouko Grip (FIN) has competed in both Winter and Summer Paralympic Games, winning a total of 17 medals. His medals have come in cross-country races (both relay and individual), biathlon, and track and field events. Grip — who has **polio** in his left hand — was inducted into the Paralympic Hall of Fame in 2006.

HEAVY METAL

Lioubov Vasilieva (RUS) came away from the 2006 Winter Paralympics with four medals — three golds and a bronze — including gold in the women's 3 x 2.5km relay. Rustam Garifoullin (RUS) took home two golds and a silver, the silver coming in the men's 1 x 3.75km + 2 x 5km relay.

RACE BASICS

The men's race for 2010 — called the 1 x 4km + 2 x 5km relay — is made up of one 2.5-mile (4-km) sitting leg, one 3.1-mile (5-km) standing leg, and one 3.1-mile (5-km) visually impaired leg. The women's event for 2010 — called the 3 x 2.5km relay — is made up of three 1.5-mile (2.5km) legs. Teams must use classic technique for two legs of the race and free technique for one leg.

Rustam Garifoullin (RUS) crosses the finish line during the 2006 men's cross-country relay.

SHORT-DISTANCE BIATHLON

Accuracy and speed are key to winning a gold medal in the short-distance biathlon.

BIATHLON BEGINNINGS

Biathlon debuted at the 1988 Paralympic Winter Games with a short-distance race for men with physical disabilities. The men's visually impaired event was added to the program in 1992, and different women's biathlon events were added in 1994.

FIRST MEDAL WINNERS

When biathlon made its first appearance in 1988, the winners in the three classes contested were Per-Erik Larsson (SWE), Svein Lilleburg (NOR), and Jouko Grip (FIN). When the sport debuted for women in 1994, the first winners were Anne-Mette Bredahl-Christensen (DEN) and Marjorie van de Bunt (NED).

RACE BASICS

In the short-distance biathlon, competitors ski around a 1.5-mile (2.5-km) loop three times, for a total distance of 4.7 miles (7.5 km). Between loops, skiers stop at a shooting range and take five shots at a target that is 33 feet (10 m) away. For each shot they miss, racers must ski an extra 492-foot (150-m) **penalty** lap.

ON TARGET

Biathlon targets are made up of five metal plates in a row. Shooters must hit the bull's eye on each plate to avoid penalties.

DID YOU KNOW?

Athletes from Ukraine swept the women's 7.5km sitting biathlon event at the 2006 Paralympic Games. Olena Iurkovska took the gold medal, while her teammates — Svitlana Tryfonova and Lyudmyla Pavlenko — won silver and bronze.

LEARN THE LINGO

Biathlete — a biathlon competitor
Bull's eye — the center of a target
Shooting range — an area in which racers shoot at targets

SHOOTING BLIND

Visually impaired biathletes use their ears to get bull's eyes! Events in the visually impaired class have shooting systems that make sounds when racers aim electronic rifles at the targets.

THREE TIMES A WINNER

Verena Bentele (GER) won the women's visually impaired short-distance biathlon at three consecutive Paralympic Games! She skied and shot her way to victory in 1998, 2002, and 2006. In 2006, she became the first athlete in Paralympic or Olympic biathlon history to defend an individual championship in three straight Games!

LONG-DISTANCE
BIATHLON

In the long-distance race, biathletes must stay on track—a grueling ski track of up to 7.8 miles (12.5km)—and on target to stay on top.

Vladimir Kiselev (RUS) on the cross-country course in 2006, on his way to a gold medal in the men's sitting 12.5km biathlon.

2006 PARALYMPIC CHAMPIONS: MEN: 12.5km SITTING: VLADIMIR KISELEV (RUS)
12.5km STANDING: RUSTAM GARIFOULLIN (RUS)
12.5km VISUALLY IMPAIRED: VITALIY LUKYANENKO (UKR)

RACE BASICS

In the long-distance biathlon, all men and standing and visually impaired women ski a 1.5-mile (2.5-km) loop five times. Sitting women ski the loop four times for a total distance of 6.2 miles (10 km). Skiers stop at the shooting range between each loop to take shots at target plates. They receive a one-minute penalty — added to their total time — for each shot they miss.

THE BIG GUNS

Biathletes shoot rifles, which are long guns that were traditionally used for hunting. The rifles used in Paralympic (and Olympic) events are low-powered air guns that are safe for competitions.

THAT'S NO BULL!

In the sitting and standing biathlon events, the bull's eye is just over half an inch (1.5 cm) wide! In the visually impaired biathlon event, the bull's eye is slightly larger — just over one inch (2.8 cm) wide.

CARRYING THE FLAG

Anne Floriet (FRA) carried the flag for her nation at the 2006 Paralympics. That year, she won three medals in competition — gold in the 12.5km biathlon standing event, bronze in the 7.5km biathlon standing event, and bronze in one of the cross-country races.

A PERFECT 10

Olena Iurkovska (UKR) has a perfect Paralympic record! She won a medal in each of the 10 sit-ski biathlon and cross-country events in which she competed! She also competed in volleyball at the 2004 Paralympic Summer Games.

A biathlete takes aim at the target during the 2006 Paralympic Games.

WINNER FOR JAPAN

Miyuki Kobayashi (JPN) is one of the standouts among female biathletes. Competing in the visually impaired class, she took home the gold in 2006 in the 12.5km group as well as a silver in the 7.5km.

2006 PARALYMPIC CHAMPIONS: WOMEN: 10km SITTING: OLENA IURKOVSKA (UKR)
12.5km STANDING: ANNE FLORIET (FRA)
12.5km VISUALLY IMPAIRED: MIYUKI KOBAYASHI (JPN)

ICE SLEDGE HOCKEY

Ice sledge hockey debuted at the 1994 Paralympic Games and has been tearing up the ice ever since.

Action between Canada and Germany during the 2006 ice sledge hockey tournament.

ICE SLEDGE HOCKEY 101

In ice sledge hockey, two teams—made up of men with lower-body disabilities—face off on ice and try to score goals by shooting pucks into the opposing team's net. Players are strapped onto sledges, which are low metal frames with two skate blades on the bottom. Players use sticks in each hand to move on the ice and to pass and shoot the puck. After three 15-minute periods, the team with more goals wins the game.

LEARN THE LINGO

Goaltender — the person who guards the net; also called a goalie

Period — a section of time in an ice sledge hockey game

Puck — a hard rubber disk

STICK IT TO THEM

Ice sledge hockey players use double-ended sticks. One end of the stick has sharp spikes that grip the ice and allow players to move on their sledges. The other end has a curved blade for shooting and passing the puck.

THE FIRST MEDALS

Sweden won the first Paralympic gold medal ever awarded in ice sledge hockey, in 1994. Norway and Canada won silver and bronze.

NO WAY, NORWAY!

Norway has competed in the ice sledge hockey finals at every Paralympic Winter Games. With one gold and three silvers to its credit, Norway has earned more medals in the sport than any other country.

A NUMBERS GAME

There are 15 players on a Paralympic ice sledge hockey team, including two goalies. Teams may have no more than six men on the ice at one time, however. At the 2010 Games, eight teams will compete in a **round robin** tournament at the UBC Thunderbird Arena.

Norway scores a goal against Italy during 2006 action.

RETURN TO 'TENDER

Canadian goaltender Paul Rosen's 2006 gold medal was stolen at a charity event. It was later dropped into a mailbox, where it was found — and returned to him — by postal workers.

WHEELCHAIR CURLING

Wheelchair curling is the hottest new Paralympic sport on ice.
It debuted at the 2006 Games and will roar into rinks again in 2010.

Sonja Gaudet (CAN) releases a stone during action at the 2006 Games.

2006 PARALYMPIC MEDALISTS: GOLD: CANADA

The first World Wheelchair Curling Championship, held in 2002, was won by Switzerland, with Canada taking silver and Scotland taking bronze. At the 2009 World Championship, Canada emerged victorious, with Sweden in second place and Germany in third.

STICKS AND STONES

In wheelchair curling, two teams take turns sliding big polished stones toward circles painted on ice. The curlers—who have physical disabilities in their lower bodies—use their hands or sticks to throw the stones from **stationary** wheelchairs. Teams earn points by maneuvering their stones closer to the middle of the circles than their opponents. After eight rounds of play, the team with more points wins.

TOP TEN

At the 2010 Paralympics, 10 **mixed** wheelchair curling teams will compete in one tournament at the Vancouver Paralympic Centre.

THE CREW

There are four players on a wheelchair curling team. Each player throws two stones per end. A player called the lead throws the first stones, the second throws next, and the vice throws third. The skip is the team captain. He or she makes strategy decisions and throws the last—and most important—stones in each end.

LEARN THE LINGO

End—one round in a curling game
Stones—large round playing pieces used in curling; also called rocks
Throw—to slide a curling stone along the ice

CANADA'S LAST SHOT

At the 2006 Paralympic Games, Canada won the semifinal match against Norway by one point. The Canadians advanced to the finals, where they beat Great Britain—and won the gold medal—on the last shot!

NO ROOM FOR BROOMS

Unlike Olympic curlers, wheelchair curlers do not sweep the ice in front of moving stones to help control their speed. When players throw rocks during the Paralympic Games, there is no room for brooms—or errors.

SKIP TO IT

Chris Daw (CAN), the skip for Canada's gold medal winning wheelchair curling team in 2006, is no stranger to competitive sports. A stroke survivor, he competed in three Paralympic Summer Games in wheelchair racing and wheelchair rugby before switching to the Winter Paralympics.

A SNAPSHOT OF THE VANCOUVER 2010 WINTER OLYMPICS

PARALYMPICS
THE TEAMS

Everyone is getting ready for Vancouver in 2010! Paralympic teams are still being determined. The listings below include the top ranking nations from the most recent world championships. Who among them will be the teams to watch in the Vancouver Winter Paralympics? Visit the Web site www.vancouver2010.com for more information about the upcoming competitions.

ALPINE SKIING

2008-2009 IPC Alpine Skiing World-Cup
Men and Women Combined Ranking in Each Event by Nation

Slalom:
1. Austria
2. U.S.A.
3. Canada

Giant Slalom:
1. Canada
2. Japan
3. Germany

Super-Combined:
1. Austria
2. Canada
3. U.S.A.

Super G:
1. Canada
2. Austria
3. Slovakia

Downhill:
1. Canada
2. U.S.A.
3. Germany

CROSS-COUNTRY SKIING

2008-2009 IPC Cross-Country World Cup
Event Ranking by Nation

Men—Sprint:
1. Russia
2. Belarus
3. Norway

Men—10KM:
1. Russia
2. Belarus
3. Norway

Men—15KM:
1. Belarus
2. U.S.A.
3. France

Men—20KM:
1. Ukraine
2. France
3. Norway

Women—Sprint:
1. Russia
2. Belarus
3. Canada

Women—5KM:
1. Russia
2. Belarus
3. Ukraine

Women—10KM:
1. Belarus
2. U.S.A.
3. Canada

Women—15KM:
1. Russia
2. Belarus
3. Canada

Russian Vladimir Kiselev celebrates as he wins the gold medal for biathlon 12.5 km sitting race at the Turin Winter Paralympic Games in March 2006.

28

BIATHLON

2008-2009 IPC Biathlon World Cup

Event Ranking by Nation

Men — Pursuit:
1. Russia
2. France
3. Norway
4. Germany
5. Ukraine

Men–Short:
1. France
2. Russia
3. Norway
4. Ukraine
5. Belarus

Men — Long:
1. Russia
2. France
3. Ukraine
4. Japan
5. Norway

Women — Pursuit:
1. Russia
2. Ukraine
3. Canada
4. Japan
5. Belarus

Women — Short:
1. Russia
2. Ukraine
3. Japan
4. Belarus
5. Poland

Women — Long:
1. Russia
2. Ukraine
3. Japan
4. Canada
5. Belarus

WHEELCHAIR CURLING

2009 Wheelchair Curling World Championships

Mixed Team:
1. Jim Armstrong (CAN)
2. Jalle Jungnell (SWE)
3. Jens Jaeger (GER)
4. Augusto Perez (USA)
5. Michale McCreadie (SCO)
6. Haksung Kim (KOR)
7. Rune Lorentsen (NOR)
8. Haitao Wang (CHN)
9. Andrea Tabanelli (ITA)
10. Manfred Bollinger (SUI)

ICE SLEDGE HOCKEY

2009 IPC Ice Sledge Hockey World Championships

Men:
1. U.S.A.
2. Norway
3. Canada
4. Japan
5. Czech Republic
6. Italy

THE VENUES IN VANCOUVER

BIATHLON AND CROSS-COUNTRY SKIING:
WHISTLER OLYMPIC/ PARALYMPIC PARK

- venue capacity: 12,000 in each of three stadiums
- located in Whistler, British Columbia
- one-square-kilometre (0.6 square miles) includes three separate stadiums for cross-country skiing, biathlon, and ski-jumping
- a portable ten-meter air and laser rifle biathlon range in the cross-country stadium for the biathlon events
- stadiums are located about one quarter mile (400 m) apart
- approximately 9.3 miles (15 km) of trails for cross-country skiing and biathlon
- a five-kilometer course for the standing classes and a specially designed 3.75-kilometer course for the sit-ski classes
- biathlon stadium has 30 lanes

ICE SLEDGE HOCKEY:
UBC THUNDERBIRD ARENA

- venue capacity: 7,200
- located on the campus of University of British Columbia in Vancouver, BC
- elevation: 295 (90 m)

WHEELCHAIR CURLING:
VANCOUVER OLYMPIC/ PARALYMPIC CENTRE

- venue capacity: 6,000
- located in Vancouver, British Columbia
- elevation: 242 feet (74 m)

GLOSSARY

alpine Describing something that takes place on a mountain

amputee A person whose arm or leg is missing or has been removed

debut To perform something for the first time or the first time an event is added to competition

disqualified To be eliminated from competition for not following the rules

endurance The ability to keep at a difficult activity for a long time

interval A set amount of time between two happenings

mixed Consisting of both men and women

Nordic Describing events that include cross-country skiing (the act of skiing on flat land) or ski jumping

paraplegia The inability to move one's legs and lower body

penalty In sports, a punishment for missing a shot or failing at something

podium A platform on which the winners of an event receive their awards

polio A disease that causes muscles not to work

prosthesis An artificial body part, such as an arm or leg

rehabilitate To restore to good health

relay A type of race in which teams compete, with each member of the team going part of the distance

round robin A tournament in which each team plays every other team

Scandinavian Referring to several northern European countries including Norway, Denmark, Sweden, Iceland, and Finland

sighted Having the ability to see

sprint To move very fast for a short distance

stationary Not moving

sweep To win all the prizes or events in a competition

visually impaired Partially or completely blind

BOOKS

Bailey, Steve. *Athlete First: A History of the Paralympic Movement* (Chichester, England: John Wiley & Sons, 2008)

Brittain, Ian. *The Paralympic Games Explained* (New York: Routledge, 2009)

Oxlade, Chris, and David Ballheimer. *Olympics* (New York: Dorling Kindersley, 2005)

Schultz Nicholson, Lorna. *Fighting for Gold: The Story of Canada's Sledge Hockey Paralympic Gold* (Halifax, Nova Scotia: James Lorimer & Company, 2008)

WEB SITES

Canadian Paralympic Committee (CPC)   www.paralympic.ca
The official site of the Canadian Paralympic Committee.

International Biathlon Union (IBU)   www.biathlonworld.com
The official site of the international governing body of biathlon.

International Ice Hockey Federation (IIHF)   www.iihf.com
The official site of the international governing body of ice hockey.

International Paralympic Committee (IPC)   www.paralympic.org
The official site of the International Paralympic Committee.

International Ski Federation   www.fis-ski.com
The official site of the international governing body of skiing.

U.S. Paralympic Team   www.usparalympics.org
The site of U.S. Paralympics, a part of the U.S. Olympic Committee.

**Vancouver Organizing Committee for the 2010
Olympic and Paralympic Winter Games (VANOC)**   www.vancouver2010.com
The official site of the Vancouver 2010 Olympic/Paralympic Winter Games.

World Curling Federation   www.worldcurling.org
The official site of the international governing body of curling.

Printed in the U.S.A. — CG

COUNTRY ABBREVIATIONS

AUS — Australia
AUT — Austria
BLR — Belarus
CAN — Canada
CZE — Czechoslovakia/ Czech Republic
DEN — Denmark
ESP — Spain
FIN — Finland
FRA — France
FRG — Federal Republic of Germany (1949–1990)
GER — Germany
ITA — Italy
JPN — Japan
NED — Netherlands
NOR — Norway
POL — Poland
RUS — Russia
SUI — Switzerland
SWE — Sweden
UKR — Ukraine
USA — United States of America